Hamlet

For Kids

by
Lois Burdett

FIREFLY BOOKS

A FIREFLY BOOK

Published by Firefly Books Ltd. 2000
Copyright © 2000 Lois Burdett

Library of Congress Cataloging in Publication Data available.

Canadian Cataloguing in Publication Data

Burdett, Lois
   Hamlet for kids

(Shakespeare can be fun)
ISBN 1-55209-522-3 (bound) ISBN 1-55209-530-4 (pbk.)

1. Children's plays, Canadian (English).* 2. Children's poetry, Canadian (English).* 3. Readers' theatre.
4. Shakespeare, William, 1564–1616 – Adaptations.
I. Shakespeare, William, 1564–1616. Hamlet. II. Title. III. Series.

PR2878.H35B87   2000   jC812'.54   C99-932627-9

Published in Canada in 2000 by
Firefly Books Ltd.
3680 Victoria Park Avenue
Willowdale, Ontario
Canada M2H 3K1

Published in the United States in 2000 by
Firefly Books (U.S.) Inc.
P.O. Box 1338, Ellicott Station
Buffalo, New York 14205

Printed and bound in Canada by
Friesens, Altona, Manitoba

Design concept by Lois Burdett

The Publisher acknowledges the financial support of the Government of Canada through the Book Publishing Industry Development Program for our publishing activities.

Other books in the series:
A Child's Portrait of Shakespeare
Twelfth Night for Kids
Macbeth for Kids
A Midsummer Night's Dream for Kids
Romeo and Juliet for Kids
The Tempest for Kids

Robin Wilhelm

Lois Burdett's Grade 2 and 3 students

Foreword

It's very difficult to say anything original about Hamlet. Fortunately, I don't have to. That task has been beautifully achieved by this book. Lois Burdett and her extremely talented and imaginative group of children have managed the impossible: the story of Hamlet, refreshingly retold.

Having played the title role many times and directed the play on screen, I approached this volume with some trepidation. I tried therefore to imagine reading it, as some readers will, with no knowledge of the play. For many people, I am sure, Hamlet is just a famous name. There may be dim associations with a man in black tights who spends a lot of time talking to himself, and seems to have a penchant for skulls. But many will be in the state of blissful ignorance about Shakespeare's most famous play, and will be unfussed by what 400 years of analysis, scholarship and performance may have done to obscure the brilliance of the original.

For anyone coming to this play for the first time (regardless of age), or indeed for those like myself who may be dangerously overfamiliar with the work, this book is a treat.

Aside from Ms. Burdett's lucid, funny and evocative rendition of the story, there is the priceless contribution of the children. Here is a veracious thrill of that first excited, imaginative response to a great yarn. There are passionate reactions to the characters, which they draw with real feeling, and comments on the story and the people, which are intelligent, moving and very, very funny.

Fun is the key to this book. It takes a cultural icon and makes you understand its power in an effortlessly enjoyable way.

My congratulations to this remarkable group. I have only one complaint. Could they please let me read the next one before I make the film!

KENNETH BRANAGH

THE CHARACTERS

The Royal Family

HAMLET . . . . Prince of Denmark

GHOST OF
    KING HAMLET . . . . Former King of Denmark,
Hamlet's father

GERTRUDE . . . . .Queen of Denmark,
Hamlet's mother

CLAUDIUS . . . . Present King of Denmark,
Hamlet's uncle

The Court

POLONIUS . . . . King's counsellor

OPHELIA . . . . Daughter of Polonius

LAERTES . . . . Son of Polonius

MARCELLUS, BARNARDO, FRANCISCO
    . . . . Guards at Elsinore

Visitors to the Court

HORATIO, ROSENCRANTZ, GUILDENSTERN

    . . . . Hamlet's university friends

PROLOGUE, PLAYER KING, PLAYER QUEEN,
PLAYER MURDERER . . . . Actors visiting Elsinore

Others

PRIEST . . . . at Ophelia's funeral

GRAVEDIGGERS

SERVANTS, LORDS, LADIES, OTHER ATTENDANTS

Ashley Kropf (age 10)

I have a story, that is often told
Of a Prince named Hamlet, from days of old.
His troubled mind, we shall explore,
As I take you now to Elsinore.
In this royal castle, on Denmark's coast,
Nervous sentries keep watch at their post.

High on the battlements, the sentinels stare round.
The biting wind is the only sound.
For the past two nights, they've seen a strange sight,
A phantom ghost who stalks the night.
Now, it's past midnight and close to the time
When the clock tower bell will begin to chime.
So let's join these men out there in the cold,
And watch this tragic tale unfold.

Katie Besworth (age 9)

6

"Tell me Francisco," Barnardo inquired,
"Have you had quiet guard? What has transpired?"
"Not a mouse stirring," Francisco replied,
"Nothing uncommon have I espied."
But a sudden sound made him draw his sword.
"Stand ho! Who is there?" he loudly implored.
Hamlet's friend, Horatio, strode into sight,
"What, has this thing appeared again tonight?"
A guard named Marcellus also came into view,
"Horatio won't believe what I tell him is true."
Horatio laughed, "You have nothing to fear.
Tush, tush," he continued, "'twill not appear!"

Anika Johnson (age 9)

Elly Vousden (age 8)

As Francisco departed into the night,
Barnardo began his tale of fright,
"Last night before our watch was done,
Just as the bell was tolling one..."
But before Barnardo could further explain,
Marcellus shrieked, "Look where it comes again!"
In flashing armour and with stately gait,
The ghost moved towards them at a steady rate.
Barnardo trembled, as he looked straight ahead,
"In the same figure, like the King that's dead!"
Horatio did not leave his post,
He was determined to confront the ghost.
"What art thou, and who do you seek?
By heaven, I charge thee, Speak!"
But the shadowy figure would not obey.
And with a glance, it turned away.

8

"'Tis gone!" breathed Marcellus. "Horatio, you look pale.
Is it not like the King in every detail?"
"As thou art to thyself," Horatio spoke straight,
"This bodes disaster for Denmark, our state.
But behold. Look where it comes again!" he cried.
It moved majestically, with arms open wide.
Just then, the cock crowed to signify day.
The spirit was startled and faded away.
The guards decided to interfere,
Each lunged at the phantom with his spear.
"It's no use!" Marcellus cried, "for it is as the air.
And will not listen to our futile prayer."
Horatio knew what must be done.
"We'll find Prince Hamlet. It will speak with its son."

I stood my ground as a faint cry pierced the air. The ghostly figure could be seen so like the dead king. Its haunting red eyes glimmered unblinking. I shivered! Sweat poured from my brow. Fear hangs in the deepest part of my soul!
Horatio

Story: Sean McGarry (age 7)
Picture: Megan Vandersleen (age 10)

9

Within hours of the sighting on the platform that night,
The castle abounded with brightness and light.
For though King Hamlet was just two months dead,
His wife, Queen Gertrude, had once again wed.
Her dead husband's brother had asked for her hand,
And so Claudius became the king of the land.
Joy and happiness pervaded the air,
As the court celebrated the new royal pair.
Young Hamlet ached with shame and disgust.
He thought this marriage so unjust.
He missed his father and was horrified,
"How could my mother thrust him aside?
Now in his place stands a man I've despised.
To marry my uncle was ill-advised."

King Claudius

Queen Gertrude

Claudius smiled, as he looked at his wife.
He had achieved the goal of his life.
"We thank you for coming, each and every one!"
Then he saw Hamlet, "Come here, my son."
Hamlet cringed, in loathing and despair.
This was more than he could bear.
The King continued, "Why are you so blue?
How is it that the clouds still hang on you?"
"Good Hamlet," said the Queen as she drew nigh,
"Thou knowest 'tis common. All that lives must die."

My father is only two months dead yet people are dancing with joy!!! Where does all this happiness come from? My heart drifts in a sea of despair. My mother is swept in a whirling pool of lies. I hang my head and cry.
                                    Hamlet

Story: Joy McKeown (age 7)
Picture: Valerie Sproat (age 11)

Hamlet

11

"'Tis time," she continued, "that you adjust.
Do not forever seek thy noble father in the dust."
Hamlet replied, "You don't know how I feel.
My pain these mourning clothes conceal.
But I have that within which passes show,
These are the trappings and the suits of woe."
The King was impatient, "'Tis unmanly grief!
But Hamlet, I can offer you relief.
Think of me as your father, and in Denmark remain."
The Queen added, "Let my prayers not be in vain."
Hamlet muttered, "I shall in all my best obey."
Claudius smiled, "Madame, come away."

Queen Gertrude

Oh Hamlet, don't let grief touch the heart. Your father's soul marches through you. Memories will keep him alive. Don't let those moments vanish in sadness. It will kill your spirit. Tears will not bring him back from the grave!
            Queen Gertrude

Story: Sean McGarry (age 7)
Picture: Mackenzie Donaldson (age 7)

And so, Prince Hamlet was left alone,
Lamenting for the world he'd once known.
"Oh that this too too solid flesh would melt," he sighed,
"It would be better if I had died!
My father is dead and my uncle is King,
By giving my mother a wedding ring.
Within a month they married. Oh most wicked speed!
Frailty, thy name is woman! How could she concede?
These strange events, my soul have wrung,
But break, my heart, for I must hold my tongue."

Hamlet

Dear Diary,
If only my body could vapourize like a puddle on the ground and transform into the misty air. It is despicable that my mother married Claudius. He is the blackness of my soul and is not fit to wear the crown that my father once rightfully owned. My life has become as worthless as a weed. If Claudius was a seed I would never plant him!
Hamlet

Story: Brock Wreford (age 8)
Picture: Anika Johnson (age 9)

Hamlet paused, for he'd heard a sound.
He rose to his feet and looked around.
A man approached, his greeting to extend,
It was Horatio, Hamlet's good friend.
Barnardo and Marcellus were by his side.
"I am very glad to see you!" Hamlet cried.
He questioned Horatio, "What brings you here?"
"The King's funeral," he replied, his eyes starting to tear.
"I prithee, do not mock me," Hamlet bitterly said,
"I think it was to see my mother's wedding instead."
"Indeed, it followed hard upon," Horatio was contrite.
"My lord," he continued, "I think I saw him yesternight."

Horatio

Dear Hamlet,
I have some shocking news, my lord! Yesternight while we were on duty the ghost of your father rose above the tower. I tried talking to it but it would not speak. As soon as the cock crowed once, twice, thrice he began to slowly fade. All that was left was a chilling silence.
                    Horatio

Story: Piers Fox (age 7)
Picture: Erin Patterson (age 10)

"Saw? Who?" Hamlet demanded, his face turning pale
As Horatio related each curious detail.
For the Prince, this was indeed an upsetting blow,
"In armour, say you, Horatio, from top to toe?
All is not well! That much is plain.
I will watch tonight. Perchance 'twill walk again.
Between eleven and twelve, I shall visit you."
Then he bade them farewell and they quickly withdrew.
Hamlet reflected, "Foul deeds will rise,
Though all the earth overwhelms them, to men's eyes."

Hamlet

The heart and the blood
Spilled upon thy grave
Staining thy earthly flesh.
Dear father? Awake?
It bodes not well.
The visions of the mind
Threaten my very soul!
                    Hamlet

Story: Katie Besworth (age 8)
Picture: Kate Vanstone (age 10)

15

Now Claudius knew nothing of this new plan.
Neither did Polonius, the King's right-hand man.
In his job as chamberlain, he advised everyone,
Including, of course, both his daughter and son.
"Laertes, my boy, as you leave for France today,
I have some counsel I want you to obey.
Give thy thoughts no tongue. Think before you act.
Be friendly to others, and treat all with tact.
Dress, as well as you can, but keep it low key.
Neither a borrower nor a lender be.
This above all: to thine own self be true.
Farewell, my son, my blessings go with you."
Laertes bowed low, "I take my leave, good lord."
Then he hugged his sister, whom he simply adored.

Polonius

Advice to Laertes
① Keep your thoughts
   tucked away.
② Be friendly but not
   too friendly.
③ Avoid fights-Just leave.
④ Talk less, listen more.
⑤ Dress in fine clothes
   but don't go overboard.
⑥ Hold on to your money
   belt.
                    Polonius

Story: Matthew Wilhelm (age 7)
Picture: Caitlin Ellison (age 8)

16

Polonius turned to his daughter with further advice.
This time, though, he was more concise,
"What's between you and Hamlet? Tell me the truth!
Ophelia, are you dating this noble youth?"
His daughter replied softly, "I cannot disagree.
He hath made many tenders of his affection to me."
"Affection?" Polonius snorted, "Don't believe his pleas!
He trifles with your love. He's nothing but a tease.
There will be no more courting! You will do as I say!"
The poor girl had no choice, "Father, I shall obey!"

Dearest Ophelia,
I hear there is some attraction between you and Hamlet. Is that true, my dear? Do not, I repeat, do not set your hopes too high. Your payment will be sadness. Grief is worse than love. I advise you to dump Hamlet. And that is my final word!
                                        Polonius

Story: Andrea Petrak (age 8)
Picture: Robyn Lafontaine (age 10)

Ophelia

Evening finally came, and in the stinging air
Three figures on the platform heard a loud fanfare.
Trumpets and cannons marked the revelry of the King.
Drunken celebrations were already in full swing.
"Such drinking," Hamlet raged, "really is a crime.
I'm cold and tired. Will this clock bell never chime?"
Horatio's eyes grew wide. He trembled in the night,
"Look, my lord, it comes!" It was a shocking sight.

Eliza Johnson (age 8)

18

"Angels of grace defend us!" Hamlet was terrified.
But he swiftly took control, and his panic he denied.
"I'll call thee King, father, royal Dane,
Explain why you have come. What do you wish to gain?"
The spirit raised its hand, and beckoned Hamlet on.
"Don't go!" implored his friends. "You are but a pawn!"
The two tried to restrain him, but Hamlet struggled free.
"It waves me still!" he cried. "Go on, I'll follow thee!"

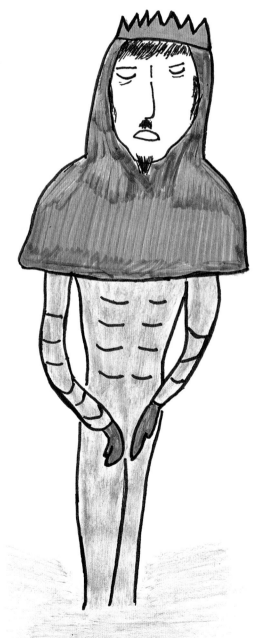

Help me dear God. What is this horrific vision before me? Its haunting blank eyes give no clue. I am trapped in a magnetic field of curiosity. Why has my father broken free from his holy tomb under the rich soil? Lines of confusion streak through my mind. Though my body commands me to stay, my brain tells me to follow.

Hamlet

Story: Brock Wreford (age 8)
Picture: Eliza Johnson (age 8)

19

Now the two stood together, royal Father and his son.
"Mark me!" the ghost shuddered, "My hour is almost come.
I am thy father's spirit doomed to walk the night.
At dawn, I render up myself and disappear from sight."
The mournful voice resounded from above,
"If thou didst ever thy dear father love,
Revenge his foul and most unnatural murder!" he cried.
"Murder?" Hamlet trembled, and looked horrified.
The very word hammered in his brain.
"Murder most foul!" the spirit bellowed again.
"'Tis said," the ghost moaned, "that a serpent bit me.
And I died in my orchard, in tranquillity.
Indeed, a serpent did sting thy father's life.
But it now wears his crown, and has married his wife."

The Ghost of Hamlet's father   20

Hamlet my son, it is time for the hideous news of truth and sorrow. It was said that a serpent's tooth stopped my life! That tall tale had everyone fooled. The reptile that cancelled my rights has stolen the royal throne. Be not mistaken by the smile on your uncle's face, for he is a murderer!

Story: Evan Ohler (age 8)
Picture: Ashley Kropf (age 10)

"Oh, my prophetic soul!" cried Hamlet, "Can this be true?"
"Aye!" moaned the spirit, "The facts I will review.
As I slept peacefully on that fateful day,
Your uncle crept towards me, like a beast of prey.
A poisonous liquid, he poured into my ear.
Then he slunk away, with a laughing sneer.
It was a moment I could never have foreseen.
My brother snatched my life, my crown, and my Queen.
Bear it not, my son! Set my tortured spirit free!
Adieu, adieu, adieu. Remember me!"

Sydney Truelove (age 9)

Hamlet stood alone and watched the ghost retreat,
"Remember thee? I will! This challenge I will meet.
Your command alone stands forever in my brain.
I give my oath, dear father. You have not come in vain!"
Just then his two comrades rushed into view,
Horatio puffed, "My lord, what did it say to you?"
"The secret," uttered Hamlet, "is locked in my heart.
I'm afraid you will reveal it. I think it's best we part."

The fire of hatred burns in my soul. Claudius is a liar, a coward and a thief who steals people's lives. Oh most heavenly angels give me strength to keep me sturdy on my feet. I will sweep away all cares and banish small thoughts. I am so out of joy! Nothing can stop me now!

Hamlet

Hamlet

Story: Théa Pel (age 8)
Picture: Sydney Truelove (age 9)

"Promise me," said Hamlet, "you'll never bring to light
The unusual events that have occurred tonight.
And if I pretend madness, and you see me acting odd,
Do not even hint you know the cause for this facade."
He pulled out his rapier, "Take an oath upon my sword!"
The Prince's wild behaviour could not be ignored.
"Swear!" cried Hamlet. And the ghost echoed, "Swear!"
The final vows were taken in this strange affair.
"Come now, my friends, let's go in, I pray."
Then Hamlet paused, his look was faraway.
"The time is out of joint. Oh, cursed spite,
That ever I was born to set it right!"

> My eyes, my ears, and my heart are weakened from what I have seen. As long as flowers still grow round my dear father's grave, his soul must be put to rest. Nothing in the history of humankind hath brought so much wonder.
>
> Hamlet

Story: Kelsey Cunningham (age 8)
Picture: Eliza Johnson (age 8)

Horatio

Hamlet

Marcellus

23

Before long, it seemed, Hamlet had changed.
The talk of the court was that he was deranged.
But he was observing the King's every move.
The murder he wanted desperately to prove.
Into Ophelia's chamber, he barged one day.
His manner wild, his clothes in disarray.
His doublet unbuttoned, no hat upon his head.
His stockings were ungartered, and not a word he said.
She rushed to her father, "I've been so afrighted!"
"I know Hamlet's problem!" Polonius was excited.
"Love not returned has caused madness full blown.
Let's go to the King. This must be known."

Oh father, the most terrifying thing has happened. Prince Hamlet barged into my chamber. His stockings streamed with mud and limped around his ankles. He grabbed my wrist and stared at me for what seemed like forever! Then he walked away, his firm glance never leaving my eyes.

Ophelia

Story: Josh Strasler (age 7)
Picture: Eliza Johnson (age 8)

Ophelia

But King Claudius was not impressed.
He was suspicious, and most distressed.
Claudius plotted, "What I need are some spies
To sniff out the truth and become my eyes!
From Hamlet's friends, the facts I will learn,
I'll send for Rosencrantz and Guildenstern."
It was hard to tell these two men apart.
Loyalty was not strong in either man's heart.
They were delighted to receive extra pay.
With the help of money, they were easy to sway.
"Go now," ruled the King, "and visit my son."
"Don't worry," they replied. "We'll get the job done!"

Dear Rosencrantz & Guildenstern,
I have beckoned you here
because I need your help.
As you know Hamlet has
changed dramatically. It is
up to you to find the
cause of this great dilemma.
If you succeed, you will be
rewarded greatly. You are
men I can trust. I know
you can do it!
                    King Claudius

Story: Brock Wreford (age 8)
Picture: Katie Besworth (age 8)

King Claudius

As the men departed, Polonius came with news:
The cause of Hamlet's madness, and the telltale clues.
The old man began, "My report will bring relief.
Since brevity is the soul of wit, I will be brief.
Your noble son is mad. The facts you can't dismiss."
Then he showed a love letter, "Take a look at this!"
"Is the note from Hamlet?" the Queen asked with a frown.
"Indeed," cried Polonius. "But Ophelia turned him down!
I'll deceive him with my daughter, and my theory I will prove.
We'll hide behind the curtain and observe his every move."
Claudius replied, "This scheme I'll allow."
Gertrude sighed, "Here comes the poor wretch now!"

Dear Ophelia,

You may doubt the world is flat,
You may doubt all books are true,
You may doubt squirrels can fly,
But never doubt I love you!

You're my golden sun in the sky,
You're my rarest fish in the sea,
You're a precious jewel in my life,
So how 'bout you just love me!

I may not be the greatest
poet but it's what I feel.
You warm my heart!
                    Hamlet

Story: Sean McGarry (age 7)
Picture: Jeremiah Courtney (age 8)

Polonius

Polonius whispered, "You should not stay.
Away, I do beseech you both, away!"
Then he beckoned to Hamlet, who was reading a book,
And approached him with a condescending look,
"Do you know me, my lord?" his voice growing stronger.
"Excellent well," Hamlet replied. "You are a fishmonger."
Polonius was shocked, "Not I, my lord," he began.
Hamlet groaned, "I wish you were as honest a man."
Polonius shook his head, "He's far gone, far gone!
From reality, he has totally withdrawn."
As Polonius departed with no more ado,
Rosencrantz and Guildenstern hurried into view.

He's gone mad, my lord
Ophelia will not welcome
his love. Hamlet will have
to learn the ways of life
and how the world turns.
It may be a bumpy ride
but he'll get over it.
                    Polonius

Story: Piers Fox (age 7)
Picture: Julian Hacquebard (age 7)

Hamlet

Hamlet held out his hand and smiled with delight,
"Welcome, good lads! What brings you here tonight?"
But just as quickly, his expression changed.
He eyed them suspiciously, "This was arranged."
They tried to change the subject, "Guess who comes today?
A travelling troupe of actors we met on our way."
Hamlet was delighted, "They will be well received.
But King Claudius and my mother are deceived."
"In what way, my lord?" The two sounded distressed.
Hamlet replied, "I am but mad, north-north-west.
When the wind is southerly," he said with a guffaw,
"I know a hawk from a handsaw!"

Rosencrantz & Guildenstern,
you are fibbing. I can see
it in your eyes. You were
sent for, weren't you?
Come now, be fair and
frank with me. Tell
the truth. Give it
to me swiftly.
Hamlet

Story: Philip Phillips (age 7)
Picture: Elly Vousden (age 8)

Rosencrantz   Guildenstern

Before they could untangle this last retort,
Polonius admitted the actors to the court.
In colourful costumes, they bounced through the hall.
Hamlet cried, "Welcome, masters. Welcome, all!
Come give us a sample. Use your best techniques.
Choose a passionate speech. A tale from the Greeks."
The lead actor arose and began with great force,
Emotion mounted in his rousing discourse.
When the monologue ended, Hamlet took him aside,
"Tomorrow night could you act in a play I'll provide?
'The Murder of Gonzago,' is the one I submit,
With a dozen new lines I've added to it!"

Ashley Kropf (age 10)

The actor agreed and went off to rest.
Hamlet was alone, and became more depressed.
"Oh, what a rogue and peasant slave am I!
My spirits I cannot seem to fortify.
Is it not shocking that this player here
With imaginary feelings can act sincere?
And all for nothing! Oh, what would he do
If he had my motive, my passionate cue?
Am I a coward? Why do I delay?
For two months now, my plans go astray.
And yet, I have the beginning of a scheme.
I'll have them perform on a murderous theme.
It shall parallel the poisoning of my father," he vowed.
"I'll observe the reactions of Claudius from the crowd."
Hamlet was convinced, "The play's the thing
Wherein I'll catch the conscience of the King."

I stand alone, a crumpled coward.
I have failed my loving father!
If the actors can express their
feelings why can't I? Tomorrow
I'll have them perform
THE MURDER OF GONZAGO.
I will watch how my uncle reacts.
If his conscience overflows
it will be absolute proof!
                    Hamlet

Hamlet

Story: Josh Strasler (age 7)
Picture: Ashley Kropf (age 10)

Meanwhile, King Claudius was still uptight.
The cause of Hamlet's madness had not come to light.
Rosencrantz and Guildenstern were unsure.
So now, Ophelia was to be the lure.
"Gertrude, please leave us," Claudius told the Queen.
"Polonius and I will hide ourselves, where we won't be seen.
I've contrived for Hamlet to meet Ophelia here.
If love is the cause, it will soon be clear."
Polonius told his daughter, "Come now, let's proceed.
Here, take this prayer book, and pretend to read."
Ophelia was confused and upset with her role.
But she knew her father was in control.
And so she agreed, though deceit she deplored.
Polonius cried, "He's coming! Let's withdraw, my lord."

Picture: Cagney Schaeffer (age 12)

Hamlet was despondent, as he wandered into view,
Unaware of this intended rendezvous.
His need for revenge continued to persist,
If only he could cease to exist.
"To be, or not to be, that is the question," he mused.
For the meaning of life had become confused.
The world for Hamlet had become a chore,
"To die is to sleep and nothing more.
And yet," the Prince mourned, "I do refrain
From the one final act that could end my pain.
The dread of something after death inhibits the will.
'Tis this uncertainty that keeps me still.
To die, to sleep, to sleep, perchance to dream,
Aye, there's the rub. It's not as easy as it may seem."

To live in harmony on this planet or to die the pangs of death, that is the question. Why live in a world with grudge and scalawags? It could all be settled with a mere rapier. But to die is to fall into an everlasting slumber. My life is full of unwanted memories. But to decide it with the blow of a dagger... Is that the answer to my misery?
                    A confused Hamlet

Story: Brock Wreford (age 8)
Picture: Ashley Kropf (age 10)

32

A sudden movement caught Hamlet's eye.
He turned and saw Ophelia standing close by.
She stammered nervously, "My greetings, I convey.
The presents you gave me, I must return today."
Now, once again, his suspicions flared,
"These gifts came not from me!" Hamlet glared.
Ophelia was confused by his change of mind,
"Rich gifts wax poor when givers prove unkind."
Hamlet now suspected spies everywhere.
He felt betrayed, and Ophelia was the snare.
"Where's your father?" Hamlet snarled in disgust.
"Get thee to a nunnery! Women I distrust."
As he departed, she let out a groan,
"Oh what a noble mind is here overthrown!"

Ophelia

My heart is washed away in Sadness. Hamlet is a m-a-d-m-a-n. His love has gone stale. One slip and it's all over. Here one day, gone the next, like ice cream melting in the blazing sun. That's why they say love is blind and they are right.

Ophelia

Story: Sean McGarry (age 7)
Picture: Eliza Johnson (age 8)

The King dashed from his hideout, "Polonius, my friend,
Love! His affections do not that way tend.
This is not madness. Hamlet's in control.
He's brooding on something deep in his soul.
Imminent danger is the outcome I foresee.
I shall send him to England immediately."
Polonius replied, "I have one more scheme,
That could explain Hamlet's actions extreme.
Queen Gertrude is the one, I believe,
Who can discover what is making him grieve.
I will hide myself behind her curtain wall,
From their conversation, we'd know once and for all."
King Claudius agreed, "It shall be so.
Madness in great ones must not unwatched go."

There is something fishy going on here. Hamlet is up to something. His thoughts are deep and so big I fear they are dangerous. I will ship him to England immediately. That will surely change his attitude!
King Claudius

Story: Matthew Wilhelm (age 7)
Picture: Mackenzie Donaldson (age 8)

King Claudius

While this intrigue was being devised,
Hamlet beckoned to the actors and advised,
"Speak the speech, but don't overact.
Perform the play, with my new words intact.
Be not too tame, nor too grand."
Then he called for Horatio to lend a hand.
"Help me observe the King tonight.
Note if the words, his conscience will ignite.
If he shows no guilt, as the crime is revealed,
The spirit ghost is a liar and I will yield.
But quick, get you a place. Here comes the play!"
The Queen implored, "Hamlet, sit by me, I pray."
But he joined Ophelia, who was astounded.
"The Murder of Gonzago," the trumpets sounded.

Ashley Kropf (age 10)

35

The Prologue entered, "For us and for our tragedy,
We beg your hearing patiently."
The audience was hushed, awaiting the first scene.
Two actors appeared dressed like a king and queen.
"It's been thirty years," the Player King recited,
"Since we two fell in love and in marriage united.
But, I must leave thee, love, and shortly too,
For I am sick. A new husband you'll pursue."

Dear Player Queen,
For thirty years we have
shared our life together.
A band of light bonds us
two-in-one. Many times
we have embraced but I
fear the end is near. I am
very sick. My face is as
pale as a cloudy day in
June. When I am gone you
will find another husband.
Mark my words.
            The Player King

Story: Brock Wreford (age 8)
Picture: Elly Vousden (age 8)

Player King

The Player Queen protested, "Don't let me hear the rest.
Such love must needs be treason in my breast.
In second husband, let me be accurst;
None wed the second but who killed the first."
The Player King replied, "You'll break your vow,
Though I'm certain you believe what you say now."
The Player Queen moaned, "Pursue me lasting strife,
If, once a widow, ever I be a wife!"

Player Queen

Dear Player King,
Oh my Gonzago. You are such
a noble ruler, a king blessed.
I'll make a vow to break
all vows. I will never marry!
Not on your life. So let
our love be locked together
and never find the key.
        The Player Queen

Story: Sean McGarry (age 7)
Picture: Elly Vousden (age 8)

Hamlet turned to his mother, "How do you like the play?"
Gertrude answered, "The lady doth protest too much, I say."
"Oh, but she'll keep her word!" Hamlet replied.
"Do you know the plot?" King Claudius cried.
"What's the name of this play?" he continued in a flap.
Hamlet confided, "It's called, 'The Mousetrap.'
The murder took place in Vienna, in real life.
Gonzago's the Duke's name, Baptista is his wife.
But here comes Lucianus, nephew to the King.
Look, he seems to be clutching something."
Lucianus held the poison, from midnight weeds collected,
With witches' spell thrice blasted, thrice infected.

Hamlet could not keep his excitement down,
"See, how he poisons Gonzago for the crown.
And he'll gain the wife of Gonzago soon!"
King Claudius rose up like a typhoon.
His eyes blazed with fury. His face turned grey.
"Give me some light!" he bellowed. "Away!"
"How fares my lord?" the Queen tried to inquire.
"What?" breathed Hamlet. "Frighted with false fire?"
All was confusion, courtiers rushing everywhere.
The play was forgotten in this frantic affair.
The cause of the King's anger was unknown.
Hamlet and Horatio were left alone.
The Prince confided, "The ghost did not lie!
We now have proof we can't deny."

My plan has succeeded. King Claudius leapt from his seat bellowing for the play to end! His mouth hung open in absolute terror. Horror flooded his guilty eyes. Then he stumbled out of the room like the rat he is. The taste of victory was in my grasp.

Hamlet

Story: Brock Wreford (age 8)
Picture: Eliza Johnson (age 8)

As the two stood talking, in a state of unrest,
Rosencrantz and Guildenstern arrived with a request.
"My lord," Guildenstern began, "The Queen is upset,
And the good King Claudius is angrier yet.
Your shocking behaviour, Gertrude wishes to review."
Rosencrantz added, "She must now speak with you!"
"I will come to my mother," Hamlet replied.
But the Prince felt trapped and angry inside.
"Let me be cruel," he thought. "I'll not be outdone.
I will speak daggers to her, but use none."
The two devious men rushed straight to the King,
And quickly reported everything.

Hamlet   Horatio   Rosencrantz Guildenstern

Laura Bates (age 10)
40

"I like him not!" the King cried in a rampage,
"It's not safe to allow this madness to rage.
The threat of danger we must subdue.
I'll send him to England, along with you.
I'll prepare a letter without delay."
The two men nodded, "We'll do as you say."
When they departed, the King continued to fume.
Then old Polonius shuffled into the room.
"My lord, Hamlet's heading to meet with the Queen.
I shall hide behind her curtain, completely unseen.
I'll report to your Grace, before you retire to bed."
"Thanks!" replied the King, other thoughts in his head.
For the play had revealed his despicable deed,
And now he bemoaned his murderous greed.

Dear King of England

INK

Ashley Kropf (age 10)

41

"Oh, my offence is rank, it smells to heaven," the King cried.
"A brother's murder can never be denied.
What form of prayer can serve my turn?
Forgive me my foul murder?" he questioned in concern.
"That cannot be, since I am still possessed
Of those rewards for which I did the murder," he confessed.
"My crown, mine own ambition, and my Queen,
In the corrupted world, this may be routine.
But 'tis not so in heaven. There is no pretence.
May one be pardoned and continue the offence?
Help angels! My wrongdoings dispel.
Bow, stubborn knees! All may yet be well!"

I pray to the heavens. Set me free from my wicked sins. My soul is in a trap and my guilt is raining over me. Time stands between me and punishment, and time cannot be stopped. Is there any hope? I want my life back!
King Claudius

Story: Andrea Petrak (age 8)
Picture: Sydney Truelove (age 9)

King Claudius

The King kneeled to pray, but was unaware
Hamlet stood behind, his sword in the air.
"Now might I do it!" Then Hamlet paused in dismay,
"I must consider, and this action delay.
To speed the King's salvation should not be my goal.
If I kill him as he prays, heaven will take his soul.
No!" Hamlet breathed. "This revenge would be cheap.
I'll kill him full of sins, when he is drunk asleep."
And so the Prince withdrew, as the King rose to his feet.
Claudius felt clammy and was white as a sheet,
"My words fly up, my thoughts remain below.
Words without thoughts never to heaven go."

Come trusty blade. Now's my chance to slay the coward. With one blow my deed could be done. Yet he's deep in prayer. This is definitely a drawback. I shall await my vengeance for a more appropriate time.

Hamlet

Story: Alan Brown (age 7)
Picture: Mackenzie Donaldson (age 9)

Hamlet hurried to the Queen, as was her decree,
"Mother, what's the matter? Why did you send for me?"
"Hamlet, thou hast thy father much offended," she reported.
"Mother, you have my father much offended," he retorted.
"Come, come, you answer with an idle tongue!" she replied.
"Go, go, you question with a wicked tongue!" Hamlet cried.
This war of words continued, at a rapid pace.
"Have you forgotten who I am? And your proper place?"
"The Queen," hissed Hamlet. "Wife of your husband's brother,
And, would it were not so, you are my mother.
You shall not leave," he growled, "until I make you view
The contents of your heart and the inmost part of you."
He grabbed her by the arm, "I'll force you to look here!"
"Will you murder me? Help! Help!" she screamed in fear.

Fire burned in Hamlet's eyes
as he stumbled into the
room. His mouth twisted in
anger. His face was as red
as lava and his unblinking
blank stare hypnotized me
in fear. He shoved me back
into my chair, then mumbled
some words I couldn't
understand. I was horrified!
                    Queen Gertrude

Story: Brock Wreford (age 8)
Picture: Shannon Campbell (age 9)

44

Polonius was hidden behind the curtain wall,
And he heard Gertrude's frightened call.
He was afraid that the Queen would come to harm.
"Help, help, I say!" Polonius echoed in alarm.
"A rat!" howled Hamlet, as he stabbed with his sword.
"Dead for a ducat, dead!" the Prince roared.
But when he moved the curtain asunder,
Prince Hamlet realized his terrible blunder.
"I mistook you for the King," he cried in dread.
"Polonius, I never wanted to see you dead."
For the Queen this sight was hard to dismiss,
"Oh what a rash and bloody deed is this!"

Elly Vousden (age 9)

45

Queen Gertrude demanded, "Hamlet, my son,
Are you out of your mind? What have you done?"
The Prince implored, "I have much to impart,
Please sit down and I'll wring your heart.
Compare these two portraits. Open your eyes.
The one I adored. The other I despised."
He removed a chain from around his neck,
"Mother, this picture of my father you must check.
What a grace was seated on this brow.
He was your husband then, but look what follows now."
He grabbed a framed picture, sitting by her bed,
"Now look carefully at this one instead."
He pointed to his uncle, "He's like a mildewed ear.
A murderer, and a villain, who never was sincere."
The Queen interrupted, "My actions, I deplore.
You've turned my eyes inward. Speak no more."

Queen Gertrude

What is wrong with you
Hamlet? Settle down! Take
a few deeeeeep breaths.
Are you mad, man? Don't
you have any sense?
Why didn't you look before
you leaped? Oh the pain
and sadness! My body burns
with grief.
                Queen Gertrude

Story: Piers Fox (age 7)
Picture: Sydney Truelove (age 9)

But Hamlet's mood altered, as he stared into space.
A look of fear passed over his face.
For the ghost of his father appeared once more,
And his mournful words shook Hamlet to the core,
"What are you doing, Hamlet? Let your mother be.
Remember the revenge that you promised me."
But the Queen could see no spirit, just the empty air.
Hamlet demanded, "Do you see nothing there?"
She replied, "This is the very coinage of your brain.
Oh Hamlet, thou hast cleft my heart in twain."
Hamlet sighed, "Repent what you have done.
Confess yourself to heaven, and my uncle shun."

Oh Mother, don't you see?
He's right there with
eyes of fire! He glides
through your very chamber.
Have you forgotten how
your love for him grew,
like vines in the April
rainfall? Reality is in my
bones, not madness!

Hamlet

Story: Kelsey Cunningham (age 7)
Picture: Eliza Johnson (age 8)

Ghost of Hamlet's father

47

The news travelled quickly of this strange affair.
The King was terrified for his own welfare.
"That stabbing," he said, "could have been my fate!"
So Hamlet was sent to England straight.
Rosencrantz and Guildenstern were his escorts,
Commanded to deliver the King's reports.
They knew not the contents, for they bore the King's seal.
Inside was outlined a royal deal.
"Dear King of England, in return for being loyal,
I demand Hamlet's death, when he lands on English soil."

> Dear Hamlet,
> Your mother and I are sending you to England. It's for your own good. Trust me! There is no option. Go and pack your bags. The ship is waiting. When the wind catches you'll be on your way. Consider it a holiday.
> King Claudius

Story: Nicole Dunn (age 7)
Picture: Kate Vanstone (age 10)

Meanwhile, in the castle, near the chamber of the Queen,
Ophelia wandered back and forth, begging to be seen.
But this was an Ophelia of another kind.
The death of her father had snapped her fragile mind.
She was wild in her attire, her hair was hanging free.
Gertrude summoned the King to quickly come and see.
Ophelia was singing, and she sounded very strange.
The words of the songs, she would oddly rearrange.
The King was alarmed, "It's the poison of deep grief.
This is desperate madness. That is my belief."
He called to his servant, as Ophelia withdrew,
"Keep good watch of her, I pray of you."
He turned to his wife, who was looking glum,
"Sorrows appear not singly, but in battalions come."

Ophelia is acting very strangely.
Today she danced into my room,
her arms flinging in the air. Her
face was as pale as the first
snowfall. Tears overran her cheeks
and her tired eyes have lost
their twinkle. As memories
creep away there is nothing left
but madness!
        Queen Gertrude

Story: Théa Pel (age 8)
Picture: Elly Vousden (age 9)

Ophelia

49

Before the two could leave, they heard an angry roar.
Claudius shouted, "Let my sentries guard the door!"
Laertes had learned of his father's tragic death,
And now desired vengeance, if it cost him his last breath.
He smashed through the door and with sword held high,
He bellowed, "Give me my father, or prepare to die!"
The Queen restrained Laertes. The King cried, "Let him go!
I am guiltless of the crime. The facts you need to know."

Shannon Campbell (age 10)

Then Ophelia returned with flowers in her hand.
Her madness was more than her brother could stand.
She held out her bouquet to him, like a little child.
"There's rosemary, that's for remembrance," she smiled.
"Pray you, love, remember," and she let out a sigh.
"Here are some pansies, too. Thoughts, they signify.
I would give you some violets," Ophelia cried,
"But they withered all, when my father died."
She sang a few verses, then once again withdrew,
"Goodbye, my friends. May God be with you."
"Kind sister," moaned Laertes, "you I will avenge,
Your madness shall be paid with my revenge."
The King declared, "There shall be justice for all!
And where the offence is, let the great axe fall!"

My beloved sister, Ophelia
has gone mad. She is
totally out of control.
Her thoughts are locked
in our father's tomb.
My head is spinning in
sorrow. I can bear it no
longer!

Laertes

Story: Josh Strasler (age 7)
Picture: Eliza Johnson (age 8)

Ophelia

51

But the King's plans would quickly be thwarted,
For the Prince's trip to England had been aborted.
Hamlet told of the journey, in a letter to his friend,
"Dear Horatio, you won't believe the news I send.
Before we had been two days at sea,
A ship pursued us and pirates captured me.
Happily, my enemies were of a merciful sort.
When they heard I'd do them service in the royal court.
Please send my letters directly to the King.
I will join you soon and tell you everything."

Horatio, you won't believe my news. When I was on the ship I stole the king's scroll and opened the seal. A chill filled my body. Its only ingredient was cruelness. A cauldron full of letters like these would definitely keep the population down. I was to be put to immediate death!
Hamlet

Story: Sean McGarry (age 7)
Picture: Ashley Kropf (age 10)

Hamlet

The King was with Laertes, "Do you comprehend?
Your feud is with Hamlet. I am your friend.
The man who killed your father, seeks my life too."
Laertes replied, "I believe your words are true."
Then a messenger arrived with the letters from the Prince.
The King read them aloud, but the contents made him wince,
"Hamlet's back in Denmark? Is there some mistake?
But I recognize the writing. This is not a fake!"
"Let him come!" roared Laertes, hatred in his eyes.
"I have a plan," said Claudius, "to take him by surprise.
We'll stage a fencing match, for you are highly rated.
We'll leave your sword sharp. It will be unbated."
"I'll do it!" vowed Laertes, who added in one breath,
"I'll smear the tip with poison to guarantee his death."
The King affirmed, "Our forces, we'll combine,
When he's hot and thirsty, I'll give him poisoned wine."

No! It can't be true?
How can this be? Hamlet's
back in Elsinore alive
and ALONE! Has the King
of England disobeyed
my royal orders? Anger
burns in my soul. Fire
flashes in my eyes.
Hamlet must be stopped!
            King Claudius

Story: Alan Brown (age 7)
Picture: Elizabeth Farrell (age 8)

53

King Claudius

So it was concluded. Hamlet's fate was clear.
"But stay," Claudius muttered, "What's that, I hear?"
The Queen entered weeping, with sad news to reveal,
"One woe doth tread upon another's heel.
Your sister's drowned, Laertes. Ophelia is dead!"
"Drowned? Oh, where?" Laertes cried in dread.
"She was climbing a willow that overgrows the brook,
Hanging her garlands when the branch shook.
It snapped in two, as she hung her wreath,
And Ophelia fell into the waters beneath."
Laertes departed, tears falling like rain.
The King cried, "I fear his rage will begin again."

Cagney Schaeffer
(age 11)

54

Outside, two gravediggers were singing with mirth,
And telling jokes as they dug holes in the earth.
"I have a riddle," one said in a tease.
"Who builds stronger than any of these?
The mason, the shipwright, or the carpenter?" he laughed.
"Oh come now, don't look so daft."
He continued to snicker, "'Tis a grave-maker, I say.
The houses he makes last till doomsday."
Hamlet and Horatio were passing near,
And heard the laughing and the cheer.
Hamlet saw the gravedigger hit a skull with his spade.
"That skull had a tongue in it," the Prince said, dismayed.
"It could sing once and speak words profound.
Look, how this knave heaves it to the ground."

Courtney Buxton (age 10)

"Who's to be buried here?" Hamlet asked in dread.
"One that was a woman, sir, but rest her soul, she's dead.
See this skull. Twenty-three years, it's lain to fester.
This was the skull of Yorick, the King's jester."
Hamlet picked it up. This was a dreadful blow.
"Alas, poor Yorick! I knew him, Horatio!
He would sing to me in lighthearted rhymes.
He hath borne me on his back a thousand times."

Anika Johnson (age 9)

Just then, a grim procession came into view.
It was the King and Queen and others that he knew.
"Is that Laertes?" Hamlet tried to ascertain.
"The youth is weeping and appears to be in pain.
I wonder who he grieves for?" Hamlet pondered in dismay.
"Let us hide ourselves. Quick, they come this way."
He heard Laertes speak, "Lay her in the ground,
And where she rests, may violets abound."
"What, the fair Ophelia!" Hamlet was shocked.
"Was this the grave that the diggers mocked?"
The Queen scattered flowers, "You deserved a better life.
I hoped you would have been my Hamlet's wife."

Eliza Johnson (age 8)

Laertes leapt into the grave, "This site, I deplore.
Hold off the earth, till I have clasped her once more."
Hamlet was in agony, "No one should take my place!
How dare he hold Ophelia in a final embrace!"
Anger swelled inside him, like a tidal wave.
He hurtled forward and jumped in the grave.
The two stood face to face, struggling for control.
Hamlet cried, "I loved her. She was my heart and soul!"
The King roared, "This futile brawling must cease!
Depart and leave this corpse in peace."

Eliza Johnson (age 8)

Claudius continued with the evil plans he'd made.
Hamlet had no inkling he was to be betrayed.
The King requested he test his will,
Against Laertes' powerful skill.
So Hamlet agreed, though with a heavy heart.
The courtiers arrived. The match would soon start.
The swords were presented to the roll of a drum.
Excitement rose in the room, awaiting the outcome.
"Too heavy!" Laertes fumed. "Let me see another foil."
He chose the poisoned blade. To Claudius, he would be loyal.

Hamlet

Laertes

Jeremiah Courtney (age 9)

"The King drinks to Hamlet!" Claudius called, "Come, begin!"
The two darted back and forth. "A hit!" Hamlet cried. "I win!"
"Well done!" the King cheered. "Hamlet, this pearl is thine!"
Then he dropped the poisoned capsule into the cup of wine.
The King raised the goblet, "Come, quench your thirst!"
"Not now," Hamlet replied. "I'll play this next bout first."
They began to fence once more and again he scored a hit.
Laertes merely smiled, "A touch I do admit."
The Queen raised the cup, "I drink to my son's success."
"Gertrude, that's for Hamlet!" the King cried in distress.
She began to sip his drink, "I pray you, pardon me."
The King watched in horror. There was no remedy.

Sound the trumpets!
Bang the drums! Fire
the cannons! Hamlet has
scored a hit! He fights
like a pro. Hamlet, this
precious pearl is yours.
It represents all the
kingdom. Good Hamlet,
come and drink!
King Claudius

Story: Matthew Wilhelm (age 7)
Picture: Elly Vousden (age 9)

60

Laertes was now in a frenzied state,
And lunged towards Hamlet, in seething hate.
Hamlet felt the wound and was horrified.
The sword was razor sharp, and he had been belied.
Hamlet knocked the sword out of Laertes' hand,
Then grabbed it up. Now, he was in command.
"Part them! They are incensed," the King cried in alarm.
The Prince charged at Laertes and stabbed him in the arm.

Hamlet

Laertes

61

Anika Johnson (age 9)

The Queen reeled towards them and began to sway.
"What's wrong with you, Mother? What ails you, I say?"
"She swoons at the blood," the King shouted in dread.
"No! No! I am poisoned!" and Gertrude fell down dead.
"Lock the door!" yelled Hamlet. "A traitor's in this room!"
"It is here," moaned Laertes, with a cry of doom.
"Hamlet, thou art slain. The instrument is in thy hand.
Unbated and envenomed, just as the King planned.
No medicine in the world can set you free.
And the foul trick has turned itself on me."
"Then, venom do thy work," Prince Hamlet roared.
And he pierced the King, with the poisoned sword.
"He is justly served," said Laertes with a sigh.
"Exchange forgiveness, Hamlet. Now is my time to die."

Hamlet! Beware the drink!
It has been laced with
poison. Do not believe
your uncle. My life has
ended. I will never again
see your sweet face or
touch your delicate hands.
Why do I die so
unsatisfied? I repeat, the
drink has been poi...
(But her words were cut off
by death's fiery grip)

QUEEN GERTRUDE

62   *Story: Brock Wreford (age 8)   Picture: Théa Pel (age 8)*

All was silent, as Hamlet looked around.
In Horatio's arms, he slumped to the ground.
"They are gone, dear friend, and I will soon be too.
To tell my story now rests with you.
Give motives for my actions. Tell of this fatal blow,
Grieve for me awhile. I die, Horatio."
His friend wept tears of love, "And so, we two must part."
He embraced the body, "Now cracks a noble heart.
Good night, sweet Prince. I'll honour your bequest
And flights of angels sing thee to thy rest!"

Anika Johnson (age 9)

Parents and Educators

This book can be used for a variety of activities, either at home or in the classroom. Here are a few suggestions you may find helpful.

- Locate Denmark on a map of the world.

- Assemble a glossary of words from the play (for example, battlement, sentry, fishmonger).

- Post a Shakespearean Quote for the Day (for example, "To be, or not to be, that is the question").

- Write a diary for Hamlet, adding to it daily.

- Debate whether Hamlet is really mad or is pretending madness. Have individuals or groups take each side of the argument.

- Publish a court newspaper, recording important events at Elsinore.

- Create a tableau (a "frozen picture") of a particular scene.

- List examples of parental advice to children. Survey and tally for most frequent advice, and graph the results. Compare your examples with those of Polonius to his son, Laertes.

- Discuss the qualities of a good friend. Compare Hamlet's friendship with Horatio versus his friendship with Rosencrantz and Guildenstern.

- Choreograph the sequence of moves for the duel between Hamlet and Laertes.

- At the conclusion of the play, hold a press conference with Horatio.

Robin Wilhelm, The Beacon Herald

Matt Hunt (age 8)

Educators who wish to stage performances of *Hamlet for Kids* should contact the author to request permission:

Fax: (519) 273-0712
E-mail: lburdett@orc.ca

Special thanks to Ann Stuart for her friendship, kind assistance, and interest in the book.

Front cover: Anika Johnson (age 9)
Ashley Kropf (age 10)
Title page: Ashley Kropf (age 10)
Back cover picture: Sydney Truelove (age 7)
Back cover story: Caitlin Ellison (age 7)